W9-AVM-433

The American Revolution from A to Z

OFFICIALLY WITHDRAWN
FROM TIMBERLAND
REGIONAL LIBRARY

Timberland Regional Library Service Center
415 Tumwater Blvd. SW
Tumwater, WA 98501

JAN 8 2010

The American Revolution from A to Z

By Laura Crawford

Illustrated by Judith Hierstein

PELICAN PUBLISHING COMPANY

GRETNA 2009

For Mom, Dad, Linda, and Maureen—
the best family anyone could ask for—L. C.

Copyright © 2009
By Laura Crawford

Illustrations copyright © 2009
By Judith Hierstein
All rights reserved

The word "Pelican" and the depiction of a pelican are trademarks
of Pelican Publishing Company, Inc., and are registered in the
U.S. Patent and Trademark Office.

Library of Congress Cataloging-in-Publication Data

Crawford, Laura.
    The American Revolution from A to Z / by Laura Crawford ; illustrated by Judith Hierstein.
        p. cm.
    ISBN 978-1-58980-515-6 (hardcover : alk. paper) 1. United States—History—Revolution,
1775-1783—Juvenile literature. 2. Alphabet books—Juvenile literature. I. Hierstein, Judy. II.
Title.
    E208.C735 2009
    973.3—dc22
                                            2009003961

Printed in Korea
Published by Pelican Publishing Company, Inc.
1000 Burmaster Street, Gretna, Louisiana 70053

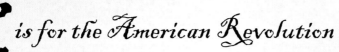 is for the American Revolution

Also called the Revolutionary War, this eight-year fight was the beginning of the United States of America. Until then, the thirteen colonies were ruled by England. Colonists fighting for freedom were called patriots.

B is for the Battles of Lexington and Concord

These battles in Massachusetts began the American Revolution. "The shot heard around the world" was fired at Lexington in April of 1775. The night before, Paul Revere rode his horse from Boston to Lexington. Some say his shouts of "The British are coming, the British are coming," warned the colonists of danger.

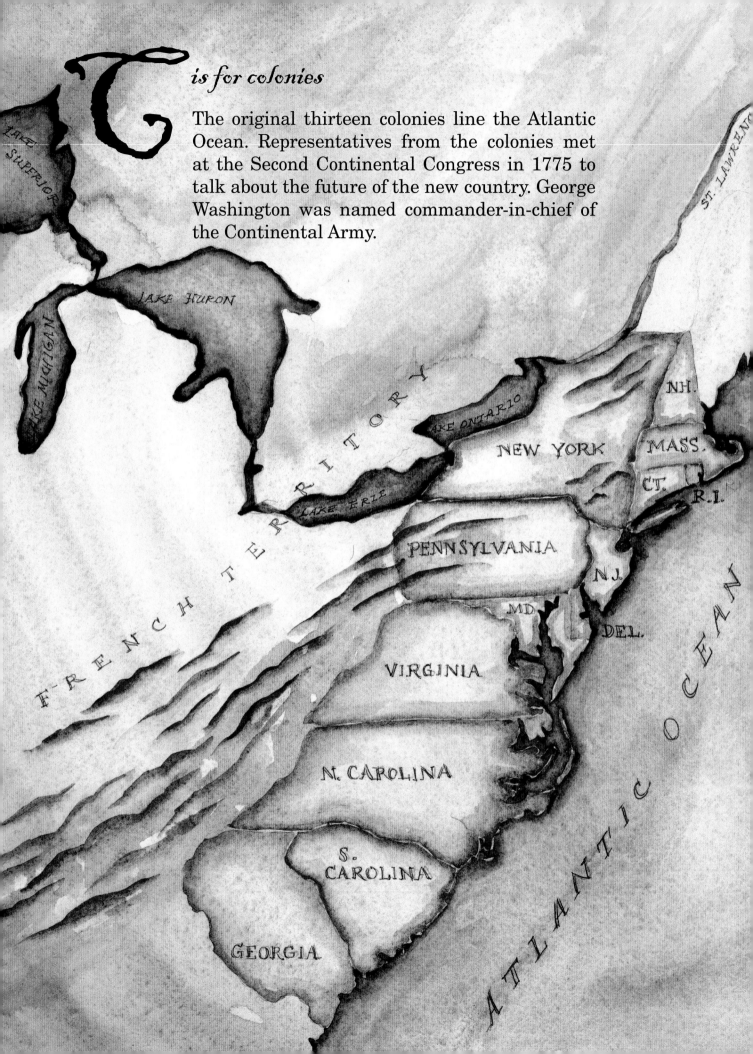

𝕮 *is for colonies*

The original thirteen colonies line the Atlantic Ocean. Representatives from the colonies met at the Second Continental Congress in 1775 to talk about the future of the new country. George Washington was named commander-in-chief of the Continental Army.

LAKE SUPERIOR

LAKE MICHIGAN

LAKE HURON

ST. LAWRENCE

LAKE ONTARIO

LAKE ERIE

FRENCH TERRITORY

NEW YORK

NH.

MASS.

CT.

R.I.

PENNSYLVANIA

N.J.

MD.

DEL.

VIRGINIA

N. CAROLINA

S. CAROLINA

GEORGIA

ATLANTIC OCEAN

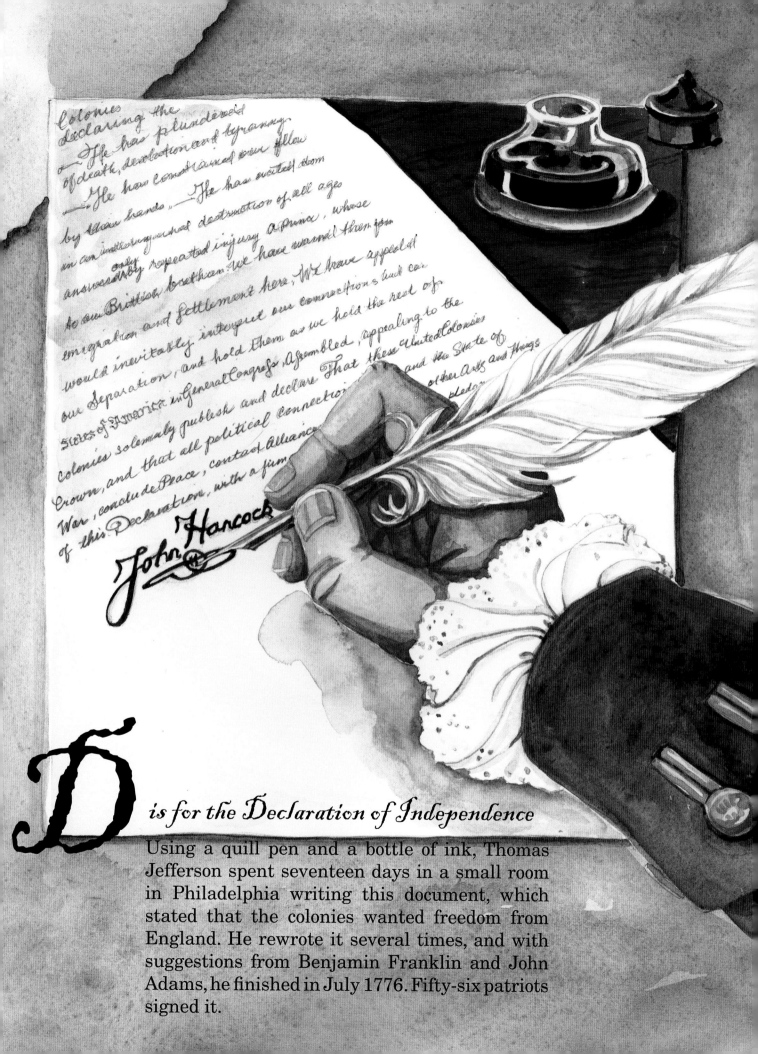

D is for the Declaration of Independence

Using a quill pen and a bottle of ink, Thomas Jefferson spent seventeen days in a small room in Philadelphia writing this document, which stated that the colonies wanted freedom from England. He rewrote it several times, and with suggestions from Benjamin Franklin and John Adams, he finished in July 1776. Fifty-six patriots signed it.

E is for England

King George III ruled during the American Revolution. England needed money, so the Stamp Act was passed. This stated that the colonists had to buy stamps to pay taxes on paper products such as legal documents, playing cards, and newspapers. The colonists refused to pay these taxes.

F is for Franklin

Benjamin Franklin was a very important founding father. He helped write both the Declaration of Independence and the United States Constitution. Franklin traveled to England and France to negotiate peace. He was an author, scientist, and inventor who experimented with electricity. Franklin started the first police and fire departments, public library, and post office.

G is for George

General George Washington led the Continental Army to victory. He was elected president of the United States of America in 1789. He did not want to serve a second four-year term but was persuaded to do so. He is called "The Father of Our Country."

H is for Hancock

John Hancock was a wealthy patriot who started a boycott of British tea. Colonists were angered that they had to pay taxes on the tea, so they boarded three ships and dumped boxes of tea into Boston Harbor. This was known as the Boston Tea Party. Years later, Hancock's signature was the largest on the Declaration of Independence because he wanted King George III to be able to see his name without his glasses.

J is for Independence Hall

Located in Philadelphia, Pennsylvania, this building is where the colonial leaders met to discuss the future of the new country. The Declaration of Independence was adopted here on July 4, 1776.

𝓙 is for Jefferson

Thomas Jefferson, one of the founders of the United States, was the main author of the Declaration of Independence and the third president. He was a lawyer, architect, writer, inventor, and musician. Jefferson died on July 4, 1826, exactly fifty years after the signing of the Declaration of Independence.

K is for the Battle of the Kegs

On January 6, 1778, English warships were in the Delaware River in Philadelphia. Colonists filled small kegs with gunpowder and sent them floating downstream. The plan was to destroy the British ships, but when the kegs exploded, little damage was done.

L is for the Liberty Bell

The Liberty Bell is located in Philadelphia. The huge bronze bell weighs over two thousand pounds and has a twenty-four-inch crack. It was rung on July 8, 1776, after the first public reading of the Declaration of Independence.

M is for minutemen

Patriot soldiers ready to fight in sixty seconds were called minutemen. Most used guns called muskets. The army included untrained citizen soldiers such as farmers, shopkeepers, and blacksmiths.

N is for navy

The patriots did not have a strong navy, but the British did. In 1779, John Paul Jones led the colonists' ship, the *Bonhomme Richard*, in a battle against a British ship. Jones' ship was hit and began to sink. His crew bravely fought. Finally, the patriots boarded the British ship and Jones took command of it.

O is for Old Glory

Old Glory is a nickname for the American flag. Thirteen red and white stripes represent the colonies. A circle of white stars was sewn on a blue square. Stars were added for each new state. Some people think Betsy Ross sewed the first flag, but it was probably created by Francis Hopkinson.

P is for Molly Pitcher

When Mary Hays' husband went to fight in the war, she came too. One hot day in 1778, soldiers in battle were collapsing from the heat. Mary carried pitchers of water to the exhausted and thirsty men. At one point, she took over firing the cannon for her husband. Women who carried water to soldiers became known as "Molly Pitchers."

Q is for Quincy, Massachusetts

John Adams and his family lived in this city south of Boston. Adams was the first vice president and the second president of the United States of America. His wife, Abigail, urged him to include women's rights in the Declaration of Independence. Their son John Quincy Adams later became the sixth president.

R is for redcoats

"Redcoats" or "lobsterbacks" were nicknames used to describe British soldiers, who wore red uniforms. Well dressed and trained for war, the British army was much larger and better prepared than the patriot army. The English also hired German soldiers, called Hessians.

S is for spy

Lydia Darragh, a brave colonist, was forced to allow British soldiers in her Philadelphia home. She secretly listened as they planned an attack on the patriots. She had to warn George Washington, so she walked several miles carrying an empty flour sack, pretending to run errands. She shared the plans with a patriot soldier, who quickly informed Washington.

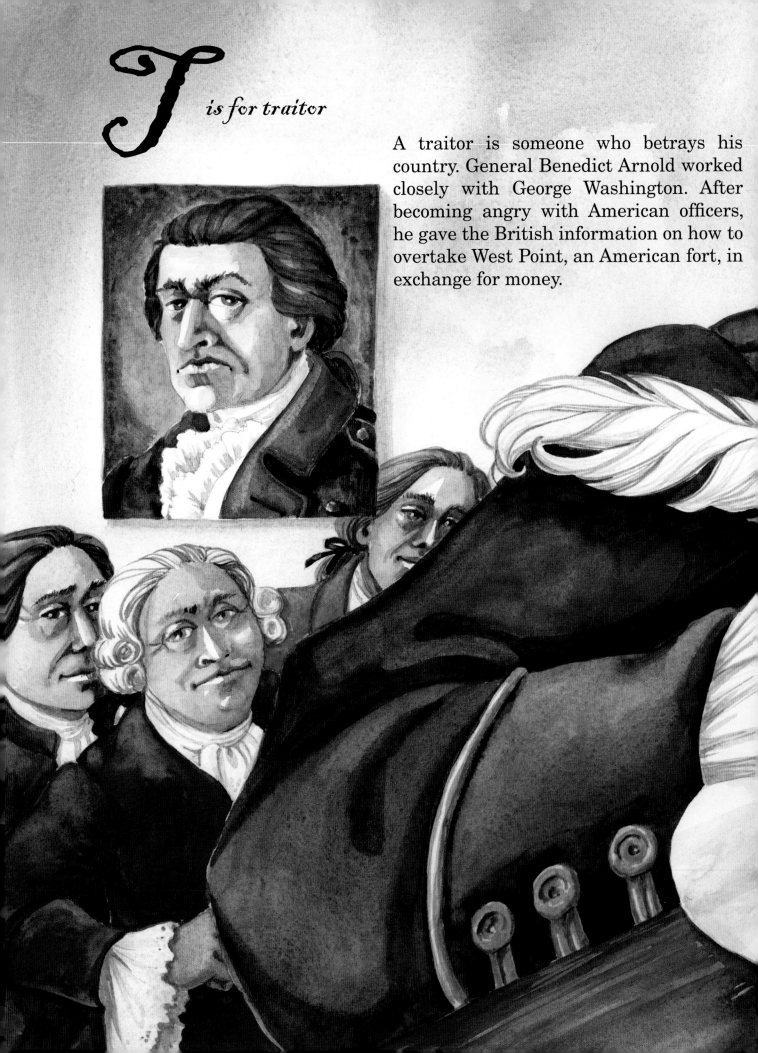

T is for traitor

A traitor is someone who betrays his country. General Benedict Arnold worked closely with George Washington. After becoming angry with American officers, he gave the British information on how to overtake West Point, an American fort, in exchange for money.

U *is for the United States Constitution*

In 1787, forty men from twelve of the newly formed United States signed the U.S. Constitution at Independence Hall. This plan divides our government into three branches: executive, legislative, and judicial.

V is for Valley Forge

Valley Forge was a camp in Pennsylvania for George Washington's army. When the men arrived in the cold, harsh winter of 1777-78, they were hungry and sick and wore tattered clothes. After several months of training here, the Continental Army was far more skilled and united.

W *is for Women*

Women were important in the American Revolution. Twenty-one-year-old Deborah Samson disguised herself as a man named Robert Shirtliffe and enlisted in the Continental Army. She continued to fight after being shot and hit in the head with a sword. When she was suffering from a fever, a doctor discovered that Robert was a woman. She was sent home from the war.

X *is in Henry Knox*

General Henry Knox knew a lot about weapons. At one point, he was in charge of about 120 cannons and 500 patriot soldiers. On Christmas night 1776, George Washington crossed the Delaware River to Trenton, New Jersey, in a sneak attack on Hessian soldiers that was directed by Knox. One thousand soldiers and their supplies were captured. Knox later became America's first secretary of war.

Y is for Yorktown

The Battle of Yorktown took place in Virginia in 1781. With help from the French, the American army surrounded the British troops. After a few days of fighting, a British band and an officer surrendered by carrying a white flag. The war was almost over.

Z *is for Betty Zane*

In 1782, British soldiers and Shawnee Indians attacked Fort Henry in Virginia. Sixteen-year-old Betty Zane ran back to her cabin to get more gunpowder for the patriots. The British and Indians realized what she was doing and shot at her. She returned safely with the gunpowder, which helped the patriots win one of the final battles of the American Revolution.